AF579494

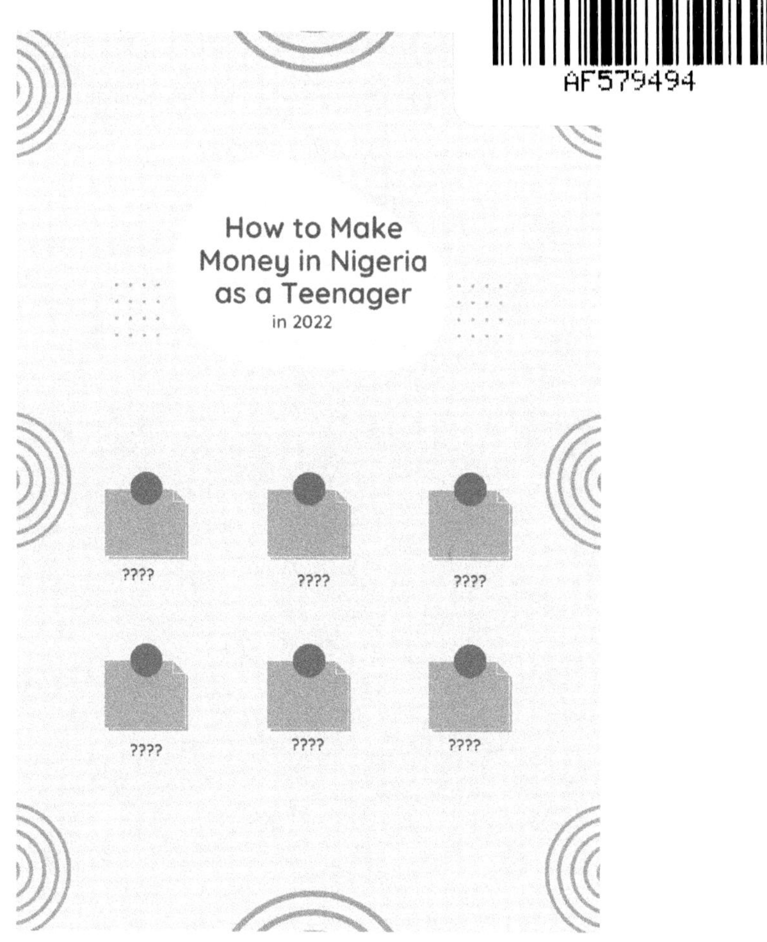

Chinazunwa Anyaeji

ISBN:9798352454862

DEDICATION

This book is dedicated to all my family members, friends and most Especially my dad who helped me in some directions by name Kenneth Anyaeji.

CONTENTS

Here are the ways how to make money as a Nigerian teenager;

Start A Niche Blog
Become an Apprentice
Learn Tailoring
Start A YouTube Channel
Start Farming
Learn Photography
Get Scholarships
Become A Social Media Influencer
Become A DJ
Learn Graphic Design
Become a Hairdresser
Learn Makeup
Sell Stuff at School
Wash Cars
Freelance Writing
Baking and Pastries

ACKNOWLEDGMENTS

9 Easy Ways to Make Money as a Teenager in Nigeria

Many of the guidelines online will tell you to buy an eBook or give you suggestions that are not Nigerian-based.

In this post, I will walk you through ways to learn how to make money as a Nigerian teenager.

It is necessary to learn how to generate income as a teenager. Trust me. You are not too young to make money.

Starting early now to gain financial knowledge and skills will make you rich in the long run.

Do not get carried away by teenagers doing yahoo in your neighborhood.

The money they get is temporary and useless. Yahoo boys and girls don't end well.

Learning a high-paying skill will give you financial stability for the rest of your life.

You will have peace of mind throughout your life because your source of money is legit.

Let me know in the comment box below if you need mentorship on the ways to make money.

I will provide further guidance to you free of charge to succeed as a Nigerian teenager.

Start A Niche Blog

A person typing on a laptop computer
Starting a niche blog is the best way to make money in Nigeria as a teenager.

Blogging is the skill of writing articles for people to read online. You can write on any topic that you know.

For example, if you are a tech enthusiast, you can launch a technology blog.

You must first identify a topic that you want to write about before you start a niche blog.

A niche blog is a blog that is about one topic.

Starting a niche blog will cost you about five thousand naira for web hosting and domain name.

You would also need to learn how to set up your blog on WordPress to start blogging.

The best way to make money as a teenage blogger is through Google AdSense.

Let me know in the comment box to get the guide to starting a successful niche blog.

Become an Apprentice

Nigerian man selling shoes
Apprenticeship is a common way to make money in Nigeria as a teenager.

Many teenagers are doing apprentices in workshops all over Nigeria.

Apprenticeship is the practice of learning a business or skill with a professional.

The time to complete an apprenticeship can be from one (1) to five (5) years.

For example, your parents can register you as an apprentice in a tailoring store for two years.

In these two years, you will learn how to become a professional fashion designer.

Tailoring, mechanic repair, business, etc., are popular areas of apprenticeship in Nigeria.

Learn Tailoring

Nigerian woman sewing
Learning how to sew cloth is a profitable way to make money as a Nigerian teenager.

Fashion design is a high-paying skill in Nigeria today.

Everybody loves to wear beautiful attire to marriage and other kinds of ceremonies.

A fashion school is the best place to learn fashion design. Also, your parents can register you with a tailor in your area.

Making money as a fashion designer is a long-term goal.

What I mean is that you may not get plenty of money as an apprentice. But, money will come after you finish your training as a tailor.

Tell your parents of your interest in tailoring to get registered at a fashion school.

Start A YouTube Channel

black dslr camera taking photo
Starting a YouTube channel can give you lots of money as a secondary school student in Nigeria.

Today, many teenagers are earning dollars on YouTube.

How it works is that you make money when people watch your videos on YouTube.

Finding your passion is the key to becoming a successful YouTuber.

You must know your spark. I mean that thing that people find exciting about you.

Comedy, dance tutorials, food Vlogging, etc., are common YouTube niches for Nigerians.

Your goal as a YouTuber will be to get 1,000 subscribers and 4,000 watch hours within your first year to make money.

9 Easy Ways to Make Money as a Teenager in Nigeria
Start Farming

Nigerian man in the farm
Farming is a profitable venture in Nigeria for teenagers and adults.

Few teenagers know that they can make money by farming.

Fish, snail and vegetable farming are some profitable types of farming.

I remember as a teenager how I made a lot of money on my parent's farm.

Depending on your location, you can go into the planting of farm products like vegetables.

You can rear birds like chicken to sell during the festive period.

Also, dog breeding is now a popular way to make cool cash in Nigeria.

Identify the kind of farming that is possible in your house.

Make adequate findings and get capital from your parents.

Learn Photography

Nigerian photographer
Photography is a way to make money as a teenager in Nigeria.

Everybody loves to take studio pictures for their birthdays and other celebrations.

A studio picture goes for about one thousand nairas in most places in Nigeria.

Many people are making a living in the photography business.

The best part about the skill is that you can continue to make money when you enter a higher institution.

You can learn photography from a photo studio in your area. Inform your parents of your love for photography.

As a teenager, it is not compulsory to get a digital camera. You will make use of the equipment at the place for your apprentice.

Get Scholarships

Nigerian student

Winning a scholarship as a secondary or university student is the easiest way to make money.

There are plenty of scholarship opportunities for young students in Nigeria.

Many scholarships pay above one hundred thousand naira to scholastic students every year.

The first step to winning a scholarship is to get a reliable scholarship update.

Join my scholarship WhatsApp group by clicking on the button below.

Join Scholarship Group Now

Become A Social Media Influencer

Nigerian man dancing

Becoming a social media influencer is now a popular way for teenagers to make money online.

A social media influencer is a person that has a large followership on social media apps.

These people offer something interesting to their followers to be popular. It could be that they have good dancing skills.

Thanks to the TikTok app, teenagers can now turn into celebrities overnight.

Brands in Nigeria love to work with social media influencers as they bring in more sales.

For example, it is social media influencers who promote many of the popular songs you hear today.

You must post pictures and videos that people find interesting to be an influencer.

You can become an influencer on Twitter by posting memes and philosophical tweets.

Become A Music DJ

music DJ
Being a music DJ is a way of making money for teenagers in Nigeria.

A DJ is a person that plays a good collection of music at ceremonies.

The services of a music DJ are in hot demand in Nigeria.

Every party organizer invites a DJ to bring life to the party. There cannot be a ceremony without the presence of a DJ.

Do you love music?

You can become a music DJ by learning under the guidance of a successful DJ in your area.

Learn Graphic Design

A person using a laptop
Graphic design is a soft skill to make money at a young age for Nigerians.

The demand for graphic designers is high now more than ever before in the world.

Graphic designers are people that create posters, logos, etc.

The church program posters that you see in your area are the creation of a graphic designer.

You can learn graphic design online on YouTube.

But, as a Nigerian teenager, it is better to learn from a computer center in your area.

Your parents can enroll you to learn graphic design during the holidays.

Become a Hairdresser

Nigerian hair stylist
Hairdressing is a profit-making skill for teenagers in Nigeria to make money.

Becoming a hairstylist will give you money daily.

No matter the economic situation, ladies must plait their hair to look beautiful.

As a hairstylist, you can make money making hair for people.

Also, you can make money from the skill when you get into University.

There are also opportunities to travel overseas as a hairstylist.

Hairdressing can take you up to six months to learn.

Your parents will register you as an apprentice in a hair salon in your area.

You must settle down and learn hairdressing with commitment.

Learn Makeup

woman in a white flora dress
Makeup is a high-paying skill to learn as a teenager in Nigeria.

Young ladies in Nigeria love to wear makeup for an outing. They pay makeup artists to paint their faces on special occasions.

You can learn makeup to make money as a teenager.

Tell your parents of your interest in makeup. They will register you in a makeup studio in your area.

It will take you six months to complete your training as a makeup artist.

Sell Stuff at School

clothes for sale

Selling stuff at school is a profitable way to make money as a secondary school student.

You can sell all kinds of legal stuff at your secondary school to make money.

Identify what students in your school like to buy and sell to them.

For example, you can do business with a phone accessory store in your area.

You sell an AirPod for three thousand naira that you got for two thousand and five hundred naira. Your gain will be five hundred naira.

It is necessary to sell legal things. You don’t want to end up in prison for selling illegal or stolen items.

Wash Cars

Nigerian man washing car
Washing cars is an opportunity to make money as a teenager.

You can offer to wash cars on weekends.

Tell car owners in your area that you are willing to wash their cars at a cheap rate.

Some people who know you well will allow you to wash their cars.

You must be a responsible teenager in your area to land this job as a car washer.

Freelance Writing

A student with a laptop
Freelance writing is a high-paying skill to make money online as a teenager.

You can develop your writing skill and offer your service online.

People on the internet are willing to pay you to write articles for them.

You must learn how to write plagiarism and error-free articles.

You will make more money as you get better at writing.

Upwork is the most popular platform to make money writing as a Nigerian teenager.

Baking and Pastries
cake

Learning how to bake a cake, cupcakes, and other pastries will give you money as a teenager.

Teenagers like to eat sweet pastries. You can make and sell cakes and small chops to students in your school.

Learning how to make cake is as simple as ABC. You can learn the skill online or register at a catering school.

I would love to hear from you in the comment box. Ask me questions where you need further clarification.

I will provide you with guidance on how to start making money as a teenager in Nigeria.

Join my Facebook page for more interactive discussions.
Click he

I am Ivar Chinazunwa Anyaeji ikechukwu from Anambra state Aguata Nkpologwu. I'm a student of Aguata high school Aguata. I live in Nkpologwu,I do many business like Affiliate Marketing, trading,etc.

www.ingramcontent.com/pod-product-compliance
Lightning Source LLC
LaVergne TN
LVHW020547160826
845677LV00015B/4239

* 9 7 9 8 3 5 2 4 5 4 8 6 2 *